# Resolution Costs and the Business Cycle

**Abstract**

There are a number of factors that may contribute to the cost of resolving a failed bank. In this paper we study the behavior of the costs of resolving a failed bank as those costs change over the business cycle. We find evidence that the costs are related to the state of the business cycle. Both the contraction and the expansion that preceded it appear to be important in explaining the loss that the FDIC experiences when a bank fails. In addition, a number of other bank-specific variables appear to be linked to loss rates for a failed institution.

# I.  Introduction

Banks play an important role that both affects and is affected by changes in the economic environment.  Starting with Bernanke (1983), there has been a great deal of work on the economic impact of bank closures.  This credit channel literature examines the effect of banks exacerbating an economic downturn by contracting credit at the same time that the economy in general is contracting.  There has also been some recent work looking at the effect on banks' probability of failure when the economy turns down.  A failure usually represents a loss to the stockholders, debt holders, uninsured depositors, and the deposit insurance system.  An important related question to the effect of macroeconomics on the probability of failure is the effect of those same cyclical forces on the loss rate when a bank fails.

There is an increasing interest in the relationship between business cycles and banks. The new Basel Capital accord is considering allowing credit risk modeling to be incorporated into the capital requirements.  Since most of these models assume independent distributions on the probability of default and the loss given default, the question has come up as to whether these two important factors could be correlated and whether economic trends play a part.  If economic trends affect both the probability of default and the recovery rate given default, then the credit risk models may be underestimating the necessary level of capital.  In addition, if default rates and recovery rates are both tied to economic trends, then capital requirements may rise at a time when the economy is contracting, intensifying concerns over the procyclicality of capital requirements if the effect turns out to be large.

This study examines the effect of business cycles on the cost of resolving a failed bank. While the primary focus is on estimating the expected loss from a bank failure, we have made an effort to formulate a model that could be used predictively — a model which, for example,

3

could be used to calculate an aggregate expected loss rate on a category of banks. As there is no previous literature specifically examining the effect of the business cycle on the resolution costs of failed banks, the following section covers previous work that has been done on topics of estimating losses from bank failures, the correlation between default probabilities and recovery rates, and the relationship between the business cycle and bank failures. The third section on empirical analysis contains information about the data and the empirical results on the loss rates for failed banks. Section IV highlights the results and conclusions.


## II.   Background

Altman et al. (2002) looked at the cyclicality of recovery rates and defaults on bonds. The authors were interested in how a negative relationship between recovery rates and default rates would affect credit risk models and, therefore, on the required capital levels. They found a clear relationship between default rates and recovery rates for bonds, with bond default rates influencing bond recovery rates. They had less success predicting recovery rates based on macroeconomic variables rather than bond default rates.

In a related exercise, Frye (2000) also found a relationship between the probability of default and the losses given default on bonds. Using a data set that included the probabilities of default for all of the Moody's bond rating categories and the recovery rates stratified by seniority between 1983 and 1997, he estimated and parameterized a systemic risk factor. This systematic risk factor had an effect on both the default rates and recovery rates on bonds. The default probabilities and losses given default for the years 1998-1999 were used as an out-of-sample check on the model, and the predicted negative relationship between default probability and recovery rate was consistent for this sample as well. From the perspective of managing risk to the deposit insurance funds, any relationship between the probability of bank failures and the loss given failure would be an important area to explore.

Also, estimating the loss that occurs when a bank has failed is an issue that comes up repeatedly within the broader topics of fair pricing for deposit insurance, depositor discipline, and the "least cost resolution" test that the FDIC uses to determine resolution method.

There have been several previous studies that have attempted to explain the differences across banks in the costs of resolving failed banks. The literature on estimating loss rates started with Bovenzi and Murton (1988). They had access to data on the actual and expected recoveries and liquidation costs for 218 small banks that failed in 1985 and 1986; they then combined this data with examination data that measured the quality of the assets of the failed bank to estimate losses.[1] The resolution costs for these failed banks were approximately 30 percent of the banks' assets. They modeled resolution costs as a function of the measures of asset quality, controls for bank size, location, and fraud, which improved the estimation results. They were able to explain about 56% of the variation of resolution costs using the asset quality and other controls for their sample.

Christopher James (1991) modeled the dollar value of the loss on assets of failed banks in the 1985 to 1988 period. He also used the classification of assets by the examiners to measure the quality of the assets in failed banks in the sample. However, James focused on using the data on the disposition of assets classified as loss, substandard, and non-classified and whether the riskiest assets were passed to the acquirer to examine the premium paid by acquiring banks in terms of a risk premium and charter value. He was able to find a "going concern value"[2] that is lost in bank failures and that these losses decreased as more assets were passed to the acquiring bank.

_____

[1] Assets were categorized as four types: special mention, substandard, doubtful, and loss.
[2] Christopher James (1991), page 1241.

Brown and Epstein (1992) extended the Bovenzi and Murton (1988) study. Their objective was to refine the estimation so that it could be used to predict losses based on asset categories. For each failed bank they had access to separate loss measures for six categories of assets: installment loans, commercial loans, mortgage loans, securities, owned real estate, and other assets. Using these asset categories, Brown and Epstein estimated a model to predict loss by estimating the losses on each category, as well as the direct and indirect liquidation expenses for each category, and then summing the losses across asset categories.

More recently, Osterberg and Thompson (1995) estimated the costs of resolving banks using publicly available data on asset and liability types. They drew largely from the Quarterly Condition and Income Report (Call Report) to get a measure of asset quality going into a failure. They used Call Report data to estimate the resolution cost as a function of quantity of loans 30 days past due, 90 days past due, interest earned but not collected, owned real estate, core deposits, and loans to insiders as a measure of fraud. Their model was best able to explain the variation on the dollar value of the resolution cost using the call report data from 4 to 6 months before the failure. In addition to the regression using the most recent data, they also ran the same regression on data from periods as far back as 3 years, but the explanatory power decreased the further from the failure date the data had been collected.

This latter type of model, using widely available asset and liability data, is the model closest in structure to the model studied here. It is important to have controlled as fully as possible for bank-specific factors when studying the effect of the business cycle on the cost of bank failures.

Presumably, a fall in incomes and asset values associated with falling output should increase the probability of bank failures. Banks essentially write loans based on the expected future values of borrowers' income streams and/or assets. An economic downturn could make

6

the realized values of these incomes or assets lower than the forecast on a sufficiently large number of loans to increase the probability of banks failing. It would seem this same fall in incomes and asset values should affect the cost of bank failures as well as the probability of failure.[3]

While the logic is clear, there has not been a great deal of success in using the expected theoretical relationship to predict bank failures in studies of the U.S. banking environment. Declines in aggregate output have been found to be leading indicators of banking crises in broad cross-country studies, such as in Kaminsky and Reinhart (1999). Finding a consistent relationship between economic indicators and bank failures has been more difficult in the United States. In a study by González-Hermosillo (1999), adding a regional economic activity variable to the bank survival model being estimated was able to increase explanatory power in-sample in some cases. The study covered three regional crises in the United States (Southwest, Northeast, and California) and banking crises in Mexico and Colombia. Each region or country was estimated separately. She found that the life cycles of banking crises in these various locations are broadly similar in terms of deteriorating non-performing loans and equity ratios. For each of the three U.S. regional crises, there was some effect from the macroeconomic variables found in either the probability of failure (estimated using a Logit model), the survival model, or both. Overall, including the macroeconomic variables generally improved the estimations, but the effects were not systematic or consistent across the episodes estimated. Additionally, a paper by Nuxoll, O'Keefe, and Samolyk (2003), which is based on U.S. data, suggests that while macroeconomic data may improve the fit of regression models in-sample, it does not improve the prediction of bank failures above a model that incorporates only bank-specific information. It may be that the best indicator of how an economic downturn affects a bank is already

_____

[3] Kaufman (2001).

incorporated in the data collected from each bank–that, for example, a regional or sectoral downturn shows up in non-performing loan numbers. Information in the bank-specific variables may better indicate the relative quality of the bank management at a given bank than the more general information on the state of the economy. However, presumably all failed banks suffered to some extent from poor management; thus, the state of the economy may have a more consistent effect on the losses that failed banks experienced than the probability of predicting failure.

If the probability of bank failure is correlated with the cost, then this has an effect on the risk faced by the deposit insurer in much the same way that Altman et al. (2002) found that correlated default and recovery rates affect the credit risk models. Therefore, while there is mixed evidence on the predictive importance of business cycles on bank failures, it is nonetheless important to study the effect of business cycles on the loss experienced when a bank fails.

## III.   Empirical Analysis

While the primary focus is on business cycle variables, in order to get a more complete picture of expected loss rates, we must also examine other bank-specific factors that may influence the deposit insurer's loss rate on failed institutions. We used a linear econometric technique to examine these relationships and found a number of factors that, taken together, explain almost half of the variation in loss rate experience.

### Data Sources and Description

Several sources of data were used in this study. The data on the cost of the bank failures to the Bank Insurance Fund (BIF) and other characteristics of the failed banks came form the Failure Transaction Database maintained by the Federal Deposit Insurance Corporation (FDIC). Additionally, these cost data were matched with a number of bank-specific variables taken from the Call Report for the quarter before failure. The business cycle data, including personal income data at the state and national levels and information used to calculate the Gross Domestic Product (GDP) deflator, were taken from the Bureau of Economic Analysis's Web site. Unemployment data came from the Bureau of Labor Statistics. Bankruptcy data came from the American Bankruptcy Institute.[4]

*Bank-Specific Data*

The variable of interest in this study is the cost of resolving a failed bank. The FDIC's loss rate was calculated as the cost for failed banks divided by the gross assets[5] of the failed bank the quarter before failure. We tested for relationships between this loss rate and several factors that might have an effect on the loss rate, including the state of the business cycle. We used the loss rate instead of the dollar amount of loss for several reasons. First, the difference in a dollar amount per failed bank of failing in good times or bad would not be particularly informative, as total dollar loss for a failed bank is a function of the total dollar amount of assets in the failed bank. In addition, using both loss and the asset types as a percentage of assets automatically removed a great deal of the difficulty with inflation as well as the problems with variance increasing with asset size.[6] Using the loss rate allows us to better capture the relevant information in the difference in the loss rates under different economic circumstances. However, by choosing to model the loss rate instead of the dollar amount, we do not get the boost in

---

[4] From the Web site of the American Bankruptcy Institute (http://www.abiworld.org/)

[5] Gross assets are total assets with the loan loss reserve reversed. This was done so that loan loss reserves would not be a right-hand -side variable while also being subtracted on the left-hand side.

[6] The heteroscedasticity problem was handled in the earlier papers by weighting the regression by $1/\sqrt{assets}$, which also helped to ameliorate the problems with a few observations of large banks skewing the results.

predictive power from the dollar amount of asset subcategories being highly correlated with the dollar amount of total assets and therefore with the dollar amount of losses on those total assets. It also makes it difficult to directly compare our results with the results of the earlier studies that estimated the cost of bank failures in dollars. We had 1,506 failed bank observations between the years of 1984 and 2002; due to missing data and the known cases of fraud (which were excluded for most of the regressions), the resulting sample size was 1,307.

The Call Report for the quarter before failure was the source for the portfolio composition and other bank-specific data. Earlier quarters were used in the cases when a failing bank did not supply a final Call Report. We used Call Report data as the basis of the asset quality variables, because this model was primarily designed to be useful in predicting losses going forward. Thus, since examination data (the source of the data classifying specific assets as loss, substandard, etc.) are only refreshed after an exam, it would not be consistently available for banks which had not yet failed.[7] If this study is to be useful in looking at the expected costs for a possible future failure, it needs to be based on readily available and frequently updated information. From this Call Report data we have constructed a variety of bank-specific asset and liability ratios to capture asset quality that would be likely to affect the loss faced when a bank fails.

However, using Call Report data does create a problem in dealing with fraud cases. Almost by definition, if the reason that a bank was declared insolvent was due to massive and previously undetected fraud, then the Call Report values from the quarter before failure will likely be highly misleading at best. We have dealt with this difficulty by running regressions

---

[7] The examination schedule varies over the sample period and across banks but is rarely less than a year and sometimes is longer than 2 years. Additionally, in some cases, if an exam uncovers sufficient problem assets during the exam to warrant closing the bank, the examination will not be completed past the point at which the determination to close the bank is made.

both excluding the bank failures where substantive fraud was found and including an intercept dummy variable for the fraud cases.[8]

*Business Cycle Variables*

Although other macroeconomic variables were tested, the business cycle indicator with the best result was growth in state personal income. Working with personal income growth has a dual advantage in that the data are available at the state level (allowing us to capture some of the variation in the local economy) and with a short time lag (approximately one quarter).[9] Both of these qualities make the data useful for the purpose of forecasting. Unemployment rates (also by state and year) were also successful as business cycle indicators but are sufficiently similar in variation to the personal income data that using both for the same time period did not increase the efficiency of the model.

The models largely use lagged business cycle variables. The reasoning for this was threefold. First, the problems with bank portfolios usually become apparent with a lag. Second, the conventional wisdom indicates that banks are particularly weak on the bust side of a boom-bust cycle. Therefore, to capture the full effect we need to reach back before a downturn into the boom years that preceded it. Third, part of the purpose of this exercise was to create a measure of expected loss that is forward looking; by focusing on lagged information, it extends the horizon that can be forecast.

---

[8] The fraud variable is drawn primarily from internal FDIC documents such as failed bank cases. In addition, cases of fraud identified by Benton Gup (1995) were included.

[9] By contrast, both Gross State Product and personal income for Metropolitan Statistical Areas were available only with a lag of about a year.

11

<u>Summary Statistics</u>

Using data from Call Reports submitted by banks, Table 1 shows a summary of bank-specific characteristics and the macroeconomic state of the world for all banks within the sample period and for failed banks within the sample period, the data for the latter having been taken from the last Call Report the bank filed before failure. The average loss rate for the full sample of failed banks was 20.6% of gross assets. The average failed bank tended to be much smaller on average than the average bank over the same period. In order to consider the relative riskiness of the portfolio of loans, several subcategories of loans and leases were considered in the analysis. The average percentage of loans and leases to gross assets tended to be higher in the failed banks than in the general sample. The percentage of non-performing loans at 13% was considerably higher for failed banks versus an average of approximately 2% for all banks. The average failed bank also had significantly higher percentages of Commercial and Industrial loans and Construction loans in their loan portfolios and a lower percentage of mortgages on small residential properties. Both Commercial and Industrial loans and Construction loans are generally considered to be in a higher risk category than some other lending categories such as mortgages on small residential properties.

Failed banks had an average of 4.3% of their assets in Other Real Estate Owned, the category that contains real estate that has been obtained due to foreclosure. By contrast, the average bank over the same period had on average 0.4% of their assets in Other Real Estate Owned. A high level of "income earned but not collected" is often an indicator of loans that have gone bad but have not been written off. This variable runs about 1.2% of assets for a bank a quarter before it fails, which is considerably higher than the average of 0.7% of assets for banks in general over the same period.

The ratio of core deposits to liabilities is included in the analysis to capture the franchise value of the failed bank. The average for this variable is 80% for banks the quarter before they fail, which is significantly lower than the 84% found for the average bank. Clearly, the amount of loan loss reserves accumulated by a bank prior to failure should have an effect on the loss rate. Because of inconsistencies and outliers in the loan loss reserve data, we constructed a dummy variable to estimate the underfunding of the loan loss reserve. This variable was calculated as

$$\left[ \frac{\text{loan loss reserves} + \text{equity - non performing loans}}{\text{gross assets}} \right]$$ when the result was negative and zero

otherwise. Given that the dummy eliminates the values greater than zero by construction, it is not surprising that the number is very close to zero for the general sample and significantly lower, -6.5%, shortly before failure for banks that failed.

Because banks that grow very rapidly often take on a high degree of risk in order to do so, we have also included the average growth rate of assets of the failed bank two through four years preceding the failure, having removed the national trend for the appropriate years. The average growth in assets for the failed banks is 2.2%, significantly above the national rate of growth of assets. Because the national trend has been removed from the constructed variable, averaging the difference over the same set of banks gives an uninformative result of zero by construction; therefore the variable was not included in the table for the average across all banks.

To study the effect of the business cycle on the cost of a bank failure, we constructed several different measures of the business cycle using contemporaneous and lagged personal income growth and unemployment. The summary of the Business Cycle Variables in the first set of columns in table 1 is the simple average of these variables for the 19 years and 51 states (including the District of Columbia) in the sample. The summary statistics for the failed banks in the second set of columns gives the average of the business cycle variables for the year and state of the failed bank, essentially weighing the average the business cycle variables by the number of failures in that state/year combination. Therefore, comparing the summary statistics in the Business Cycle Variables section of table 1 relates the average prevailing at the time the banks failed to a more general average rate. Thus, the significantly lower levels of personal income growth for the year of the failure and the two years preceding it, would tend to indicate that the failures were more likely to occur in times of and/or in places with lower than average personal income growth. The average personal income growth three to five years before a failure appears not to be significantly different from the growth rates on average. Unemployment at the time of failure also appears to be significantly higher in the states and years where bank failures have occurred. The bankruptcy growth variable is growth or increase in bankruptcies, both personal and business, over the previous year. It appears that bankruptcy growth is significantly higher in those states and years with bank failures than on average. Unemployment, bankruptcy growth, and personal income growth tend to highly correlated, as they are all ways of trying to gauge the health of the local economy. Because of the high level of correlation between the different measures of economic health, it was generally not productive to include different business cycle measures that covered the same time period in the same regressions.

In addition to the macroeconomic variables, we have included two measures to try to capture bank health in the regressions. The problem bank percentage is defined as the average percentage of banks in trouble (those with CAMELS ratings of 4 or 5) per state and per year during the year that the bank in question failed.[10] This variable was included because to some extent one would expect the resolution costs to be a function of the relative health of the pool of potential buyers. On average at the time a bank failed, 20% of the banks also located in that

---

[10] Drawn from bank exam data.

state were having trouble. On average for the sample in general, the percentage of problem banks was around 5%. Additionally, in some of the regressions we substituted a failure percentage variable for the problem bank percentage in order for the results to be comparable to studies that use the probability of default to help predict recovery rates.[11] This failure percentage variable was constructed as the number of failed banks in a state and year combination divided by the pool of banks at the beginning of the year for that state and year. Clearly, the average for the general sample period at less than 1% was considerably different from the 6% average for the failed banks.

Size and Failure Cost

Using information gleaned from the last Call Report submitted by banks before they failed, the variables in table 2 represent a summary of loss rates across the sample of failed banks. The full sample is in column 1 followed by the sample broken down by size categories in columns 2 through 5. The divisions between the categories are based on the assets listed in the last Call Report filed before failure, deflated to 1996 dollars. The average loss rate for all the banks in the sample was 20.6%. The bulk of the failed banks fall into the first and smallest size category of banks with assets of less than $100 million. Looking at the loss rates in the table, it is also clear that the average loss rate falls as the size of the bank increases. The loss rates for each of the larger categories (in columns 3 through 5) are significantly different from the loss rate for the banks in the smallest category in column 2 as well as for the sample in general. The very small numbers of observations in the two largest asset categories meant that the difference between columns 4 and 5 did not rise to the level of significance.

_____

[11] Altman et al. (2002) and Frye (2000).

The result that larger banks are generally less expensive to resolve per dollar of assets than smaller banks is very consistent with earlier work done by Rosalind Bennett in an internal FDIC study[12]. She found that larger banks tended to have more marketable assets, and that the liabilities of larger banks tended to be less dependent on insured deposits. However, a somewhat more recent study by Richard Salmon et al. (2003) which looked only at the recent experience (1997-2002) of the FDIC in resolving failed banks found that larger banks tended to be more expensive to resolve. This latter study, because of its focus on recent failures, had of necessity, a small sample that included a large number of expensive fraud-related failures.

Regression results

The results of a number of regressions are shown in table 3. The first column has a regression that includes a number of bank portfolio variables that were dropped in subsequent regressions for lack of significance. In addition, other regressions were included to test the relative effectiveness and interactions of the variables in the model and to confirm the model's robustness to the inclusion of the banks where substantial fraud was found.

Column 2 contains the preferred regression model we tested, as additional variables did not improve the model's fit. Overall, the regression explained 46% of the variation in loss rates. While we found strong results for all of the variables included (except for the two-year lag of personal income growth), a great deal of the variation in loss experience is explained by the bank-specific factors rather than the business cycle variables.

---

[12] From a Federal Deposit Insurance Corporation internal memo by Rosalind Bennett, RE: Loss Rates and Asset Size, dated February 9, 2000.

*Bank-Specific Variables*

In order to capture a substantial proportion of the variation in loss experiences, a variety of bank characteristic variables were included in the analysis. These variables included characteristics that might influence the expected loss, such as a measure of the size of the bank, asset types, and loan loss reserving.

The regression in column 1 includes several bank-specific variables that did not rise to the level of significance. Construction and land development loans as a percentage of total loans and leases are generally considered fairly risky, but the regression did not find them to be a significant source of loss. Mortgages on properties for one-to-four families are generally considered to be very low-risk loans; however, they also did not appear to be a significant predictor of loss rates. The inclusion or exclusion of these variables seemed to have a negligible effect on the other variables in the regression, and tests of their joint significance also found them to be insignificant.

The baseline regression is shown in column 2 of table 3. The measure of size of the failed bank used here is the log of gross assets the quarter before failure, deflated to be consistent over time.[13] The size variable was very strong in all the regressions, which is not surprising given the decline in loss rates associated with an increase in size found in table 2. The size variable also helps to explain the very large intercept. Taken together, the intercept (31.2%) for the baseline regression in column 2 and the size (-2.378*natural log of real gross assets) would give an "intercept" of 5.5% loss on assets for a $50 million bank. The move from $50 million to $100 million decreases the expected loss by 1.7 percentage points.

The percentage of the bank's portfolio in loans and leases came in strongly positive in all cases. For example, being 13.8%, or a standard deviation above the average (62%), raises the

_____

[13] Using the GDP deflator.

expected loss by 1.5 percentage points. The average ratio of commercial and industrial loans and leases to total loans and leases was 27.2%. If a failed bank is a standard deviation (16.8%) above the average, the expected loss rises by 1.2 percentage points. Neither loans for construction and land development or residential mortgages had a significant effect in predicting loss rates after closure.

Consistent with other studies, interest earned but not collected shows up quite strongly in this regression.[14] For failed banks, the average of interest earned but not collected is 1.15% of assets and accounts for 4.5 percentage points in estimated loss. The percentage of other real estate owned as a share of assets increases loss by 0.77% for every percent it increases, which explains 3.3 percentage points in estimated loss for an average institution. The share of core deposits out of total liabilities was used as a proxy for franchise value, and as such it performed well. If a bank's core deposits to total liabilities were 66%, the bank would be 14% (or a standard deviation) below the average of 80%, and the expected loss would increase by 1.7 percentage points.

The protection afforded by loan loss reserves and equity to cover non-performing loans should be an important indicator in predicting loss. Our loan loss reserve underfunding variable performed well. If non-performing loans exceeded loan loss reserves plus equity by 6.5% of assets (the sample average for failed banks), then that contributed about 4.8 percentage points to the expected loss. The underfunding variable incorporates information on the quantity of non-performing loans. When the non-performing loan percentage is substituted for the loan loss reserve underfunding variable as in column 3, the non-performing loan percentage is significant and has the expected sign, but is a less successful predictor overall than the constructed loan loss reserve underfunding variable. The adjusted $R^2$ in column 3 falls to 0.41.

---

[14] Osterberg and Thomson (1995), Bovenzi and Murton (1988), and James (1991).

The measure of rapid asset growth is defined as the growth rate of the bank for 3 years prior to failure (excluding the year immediately preceding failure) minus the national growth rate of banks over the same period. It has a statistically significant relationship with loss rates, but the effect is fairly small. For the average failed bank, the growth rate of 2.4% (above the national average growth) would be an effect on the order of a 0.15 percentage point increase in the loss rate. It should be noted, though, that the standard deviation was substantial at 23 percentage points. For a bank at one standard deviation away from the mean, the asset growth coefficient would contribute 1.5 percentage points to their expected loss. Also, there were some very large outliers, for which the expected effect on loss rates was substantial.[15] Unfortunately, by including this bank growth variable 128 banks were lost from the sample due to data unavailability.[16]

We included a time-varying variable to capture the health of the banking industry at the time of failure. This variable was defined as the proportion of problem banks to all banks in the state. The reasoning was that, if the proportion of problem banks is high at the time that a bank fails, it might have an effect on asset prices. More problem banks in a state might indicate a general slump in the banking sector, which would reduce the number of potential buyers and also might indicate a larger pool of failed bank assets to be sold. The proportion of problem banks to total banks does have the expected positive relationship. With a coefficient of 0.108, if 10% of banks have a CAMELS rating of 4 or 5, then this would be expected to add 1.1% to the loss rate. However, in Texas in 1989, the problem bank percentage rose to 31%, raising the expected loss of banks that failed in Texas in that year by 3.3%.[17]

---

[15] There were 19 cases within the non-fraud sample with growth rates of assets in excess of 60% per year on average.

[16] Essentially, this variable caused de novo banks to be dropped from the sample, because they were too recently created to have the necessary lags.

[17] Excluding the problem bank percentage variable increases the magnitude of the effect of the personal income growth variables slightly (from -0.27 to -0.35 for the first lag and 0.57 to 0.63 for the averaged third through fifth

In Column 4 of Table 3, we tested a variable defined as the percentage of total banks in the state and year that failed, to see whether the correlation between default rates and recovery rates noticed by Altman, et al. (2002) also held for banks. The failure rate was positive in sign, but did not rise to the level of significance. The results indicate that the percentage of problem banks is a considerably better predictor than the failure rate. [18]

The regression model in the last column of table 3 includes the cases where fraud was identified as a major contributing factor to the failure. The fraud banks were left out of most of the analysis because of the problem of using possibly tainted pre-failure Call Report data to predict loss rates for fraud-related bank failures. The fraud dummy has a coefficient of 6.6 percentage points, so, on average, the fraud failures tended to be more expensive, than the non-fraud failures. The regression appears to be robust to the inclusion of the fraud banks--none of the coefficients changed very much, and those that had been significant remained significant.

*Business Cycle Variables*

The primary business cycle variable we used was state personal income growth. A number of other variables and combinations of lagged and contemporaneous variables were explored. Table 4 contains the results of several of the regressions. We used the one-year and two-year lags of state personal income growth and constructed a variable averaging the growth rates of years lagged three through five. The benchmark model from column 2 of table 3 is repeated for convenience in column 1 of table 4. On the whole, the business cycle variables were statistically significant. The average of the personal income growth three to five years prior to failure had a strong and significant positive relationship with the loss rates. In other words,

---

lags) and the other coefficients remain effectively unchanged, indicating that there is not a multicolinearity problem between problem banks and personal income growth.
[18] In addition average return on assets per state per year was tested as a measure of bank health instead of problem banks percentage and was the right sign and but very insignificant.

failed banks in locations with very strong economic growth three to five years before failure have higher expected loss rates than similar banks that fail in other locations. The effect of the intermediate two-year lag of personal income growth was effectively zero, suggesting that the economy two years prior to the bank failure could either still be in an upswing or have started into the downswing of the business cycle. The one-year lag of personal income growth had a strong and significant negative relationship with loss rates. So if personal income fell the year prior to the bank failure, losses were generally higher. This combination is consistent with a boom-bust cycle explanation of losses in a failed bank. If the local economy was booming three years ago and has since declined, then the coefficients indicate that a bank would be costlier to resolve. Losses on failed banks tended to be not as great if the decline in the local economy was not preceded by a boom.

The signs of the coefficients are consistent with the boom-bust description. For example, using personal income growth from California in the last few years, between 1998 and 2000 the growth rate in personal income averaged 6.5%, in 2001 the growth rate was 0.41%, and in 2002 was 1.1%. The net effect for California of the business cycle variables going into 2003 is that the expected loss rates for banks in California, were they to fail, would be on the order of 3.5 percentage points higher (a 13.5% loss rate rather than 10%).

Column 2 in table 4 contains a regression that excludes the business cycle variables. The explanatory power of the bank-specific variables alone is substantial, with an $R^2$ of 0.44. The bank-specific variables do not appear to be very sensitive to the inclusion or exclusion of the business cycle variables. This indicates that the bank-specific (or portfolio) variables that influence loss rates tend not to be influenced in a consistent way by business cycles. [19] Nonetheless, the business cycle variables have a strong explanatory effect; an F-test, comparing the regressions in columns 1 and 2 of table 4, indicates that the business cycle variables are jointly significant with a probability above the 99th percentile.[20]

Contemporaneous personal income growth has a negative effect, but the effect is not significant. Likewise, as is shown in column 4 of table 4, the states' contemporaneous unemployment rate is of the expected sign but is not statistically significant. Personal income growth and unemployment rates tend to be highly correlated and as such did not give a meaningful result if used together at the same lag. Lagged unemployment did not explain the movements of loss rates as well as lagged personal income growth. Of the business cycle variables tried in the regressions, the only one we found that improved the fit of the model was contemporaneous bankruptcy growth. Bankruptcy growth, which is the percentage increase in bankruptcies from the previous year for a state, did add explanatory power to the model. The adjusted $R^2$ increased from 0.458 reported in column 1 of table 4 to 0.461 shown in column 5. Thus, for an average failed bank with an increase in bankruptcies of 11.1% in the year of failure, the average increase in the loss rate was 0.7%. However, for an unusual year such as Texas had in 1986 with a 45.4% increase in bankruptcies over the previous year, that increase would raise expected loss rates for banks that failed in that year by approximately 3%.

The model in column 1 of table 4 may still be preferable in some circumstances to the slightly more efficient model in column 5. Specifically, by including a contemporaneous measure of economic health, in this case bankruptcy growth, a modeler loses the ability to use current numbers to forecast expected loss rates for the next year. Thus, the preference of one model over the other will depend on the circumstances and application.

---

[19] In addition, in some regressions not reported here for brevity, interaction terms between the boom-bust cycle and the two portfolio variables, "Loans and leases %" and "C&I loans % of loans," were created. The interaction terms were not significant.

[20] $F_{(4, 1294)} = 12.59$

*Effects of Time Variation*

To gauge the effects of the business cycle on FDIC losses, we took an average of the bank-specific variables for all failed Texas banks in the sample and calculated the loss rates using actual yearly personal income growth, growth in bankruptcies, and problem bank percentages that varied over time and the coefficients from column 5 of table 4. This exercise allowed us to isolate the changes in the loss rates that were related to the macroeconomic variables and the problem bank percentage over time. Figure 1 presents the loss rates that would have been predicted over the business cycle in Texas given that the other factors for this average bank stayed the same. For reference, the predicted loss rate for the average bank was also calculated using the regression in column 2 of table 4 that excludes the variables that change over time. While personal income growth in Texas ranged from -0.64% in 1986 to 7.75% in 1998, the loss rate calculated in this exercise ranged from 21.7% in 1988 to 14.5% in 1999, which is a slightly smaller variation. Of this 7.2 percentage point decline in predicted loss rates between 1988 and 1999, 50% was attributable to changes in personal income, 35% was attributable to a decline in the percentage of problem banks, and the other 15% was attributable to a decrease in bankruptcies.

Figure 2 includes a similar exercise for California. Of the 8% difference in expected loss rates between the peak of 21.8% in 1992 and the trough of 13.8% in 1999, 45% of the change came from improved macroeconomic outlook, 30% came from a decline in the problem bank percentage, and 25% came from a decline in bankruptcies.

## IV. Conclusions

The evidence supports the hypothesis that cyclical factors affect loss rates. Particularly, the boom and the bust of the business cycle each increase the fiscal cost for bank failure. In magnitude, the boom before the bust is at least as important as the economic downturn in terms of expected losses, which would lend support to the idea that the worst loans are made in the best times.

In addition, many individual bank characteristics show up as significantly related to the loss rate when a bank fails. A number of balance sheet factors play into the expected loss rate, such as riskiness of the portfolio as seen in the positive effect of an increase in the percentage of loans and leases to total assets as well as the percentage of commercial and industrial loans. Also, extensive problems with bad loans, which show up in the income earned but not collected variable and the other real estate owned variable, also increase losses. The loan loss reserve set aside by the bank before it fails clearly plays a strong roll in the size of the loss experienced when it fails. The health of the pool of potential buyers and the value of the deposit franchise also make a difference in loss rate.

# Table 1

## Summary Statistics

| | All Banks 1984-2002 | | | | Failed Banks 1984-2002 | | | |
| | Obs. | Average | Std. Dev. | Std. Err. | Obs. | Average | Std. Dev. | Std. Err. |
|---|---|---|---|---|---|---|---|---|
| Loss Rate on Gross Assets | | | | | 1,505 | 20.643 | 13.202 | 0.340 |
| **Bank-Specific Variables** | | | | | | | | |
| Real Gross Assets ($ thousands) | 219,552 | 362,017 | 5,259,243 | 11,224 | 1,506 | 159,381 | 1,039,607 | 26,789 |
| Loans and Leases % of Assets | 219,846 | 55.261 | 15.625 | 0.033 | 1,506 | 61.607 | 13.761 | 0.355 |
| Non-performing % of Loans and Leases | 218,823 | 1.971 | 2.837 | 0.006 | 1,484 | 12.975 | 8.830 | 0.229 |
| Commercial and Industrial % of Loans and Leases | 219,362 | 19.030 | 13.606 | 0.029 | 1,505 | 27.175 | 16.832 | 0.434 |
| Construction Loans % of Loans and Leases | 218,975 | 3.556 | 5.942 | 0.013 | 1,505 | 4.510 | 7.358 | 0.190 |
| 1-4 Family Mortgages % of Loans and Leases | 218,975 | 26.742 | 18.079 | 0.039 | 1,505 | 19.800 | 14.923 | 0.385 |
| Income Earned but Not Collected | 219,846 | 0.743 | 0.504 | 0.001 | 1,506 | 1.147 | 0.862 | 0.022 |
| Other Real Estate Owned | 219,846 | 0.432 | 1.056 | 0.002 | 1,506 | 4.313 | 4.601 | 0.119 |
| Core Deposits % of Liabilities | 220,210 | 83.903 | 13.495 | 0.029 | 1,506 | 79.676 | 14.366 | 0.370 |
| Loan Loss Reserve Underfunding | 219,306 | -0.048 | 1.065 | 0.002 | 1,485 | -6.475 | 7.324 | 0.190 |
| Avg. Asset Growth | | | | | 1,368 | 2.155 | 23.028 | 0.623 |
| **Business Cycle Variables** | | | | | | | | |
| Personal Income Growth | 969 | 3.243 | 2.296 | 0.074 | 1,505 | 2.225 | 2.402 | 0.062 |
| Personal Income Growth (1-year lag) | 969 | 3.257 | 2.348 | 0.075 | 1,506 | 1.804 | 2.665 | 0.069 |
| Personal Income Growth (2-year lag) | 969 | 3.201 | 2.457 | 0.079 | 1,506 | 1.697 | 2.759 | 0.071 |
| Personal Income Growth (Avg. 3-5 Yr.) | 969 | 3.017 | 1.841 | 0.059 | 1,506 | 2.945 | 1.893 | 0.049 |
| Unemployment | 969 | 5.631 | 1.807 | 0.058 | 1,506 | 7.006 | 1.511 | 0.039 |
| Bankruptcy Growth | 969 | 8.087 | 24.001 | 0.771 | 1508 | 11.114 | 15.067 | 0.388 |
| Problem Bank % | 969 | 4.819 | 7.786 | 0.250 | 1,506 | 19.893 | 11.296 | 0.291 |
| Failed Bank % | 969 | 0.765 | 2.906 | 0.093 | 1,506 | 5.913 | 6.256 | 0.161 |

**Table 2**

Summary Statistics by Bank Size

| | | 1<br>All Banks | 2<br>Banks Less Than $100 Million | 3<br>Banks Between $100 and $500 Million | 4<br>Banks Between $500 Million and $1 Billion | 5<br>Banks Greater Than $1 Billion |
|---|---|---|---|---|---|---|
| | Obs. | 1606 | 1328 | 214 | 26 | 38 |
| Loss Rate on Gross Assets | Average | 20.643 | 21.569 | 17.197 | 14.626 | 12.711 |
| | (Std. Dev.) | (13.202) | (12.888) | (14.407) | (8.941) | (12.581) |
| | *Std. Error* | *0.340* | *0.366* | *1.004* | *1.788* | *2.097* |
| Real Gross Assets ($ thousands) | Average | 159,430 | 25,702 | 214,521 | 678,126 | 4,082,732 |
| | (Std. Dev) | (1,039,925) | (20,838) | (109,949) | (147,663) | (5,449,352) |
| | *Std. Error* | *26,806* | *592* | *7,660* | *29,533* | *908,225* |

**Table 3**

Regression Results for Loss Rate on Failed Bank Assets

| | 1 | | 2 | | 3 | | 4 | | 5 | |
|---|---|---|---|---|---|---|---|---|---|---|
| | Coefficient | | Coefficient | | Coefficient | | Coefficient | | Coefficient | |
| | Std. Error | | Std. Error | | Std. Error | | Std. Error | | Std. Error | |
| **Bank-Specific Variables** | | | | | | | | | | |
| Intercept | 31.495 | *** | 31.218 | *** | 28.634 | *** | 33.038 | *** | 31.055 | *** |
| | 3.522 | | 3.492 | | 3.639 | | 3.504 | | 3.626 | |
| Log of Real Gross Assets | -2.389 | *** | -2.378 | *** | -2.493 | *** | -2.335 | *** | -2.335 | *** |
| | 0.224 | | 0.221 | | 0.231 | | 0.226 | | 0.230 | |
| Fraud Indicator | | | | | | | | | 6.552 | *** |
| | | | | | | | | | 1.648 | |
| Loans and Leases % of Assets | 0.110 | *** | 0.108 | *** | 0.170 | *** | 0.113 | *** | 0.126 | *** |
| | 0.022 | | 0.022 | | 0.022 | | 0.022 | | 0.022 | |
| Commercial and Industrial % of Loans | 0.069 | *** | 0.072 | *** | 0.077 | *** | 0.071 | *** | 0.063 | *** |
| | 0.018 | | 0.017 | | 0.017 | | 0.017 | | 0.017 | |
| Construction Loans % of Loans | 0.007 | | | | | | | | | |
| | 0.040 | | | | | | | | | |
| 1-4 Family Mortgages % of Loans | -0.012 | | | | | | | | | |
| | 0.022 | | | | | | | | | |
| Income Earned but Not Collected | 3.833 | *** | 3.880 | *** | 3.425 | *** | 3.682 | *** | 3.721 | *** |
| | 0.368 | | 0.348 | | 0.373 | | 0.347 | | 0.366 | |
| Other Real Estate Owned | 0.769 | *** | 0.767 | *** | 0.901 | *** | 0.802 | *** | 0.757 | *** |
| | 0.062 | | 0.060 | | 0.062 | | 0.060 | | 0.064 | |
| Core Deposits % of Liabilities | -0.121 | *** | -0.122 | *** | -0.135 | *** | -0.128 | *** | -0.131 | *** |
| | 0.022 | | 0.022 | | 0.023 | | 0.022 | | 0.023 | |
| Loan Loss Reserve Underfunding | -0.549 | *** | -0.551 | *** | | | -0.562 | *** | -0.535 | *** |
| | 0.039 | | 0.039 | | | | 0.039 | | 0.041 | |
| Non-performing % of Loans and Leases | | | | | 0.301 | *** | | | | |
| | | | | | 0.032 | | | | | |
| Avg. Asset Growth | 0.061 | *** | 0.061 | *** | 0.065 | *** | 0.061 | *** | 0.035 | *** |
| | 0.017 | | 0.017 | | 0.018 | | 0.017 | | 0.013 | |
| **Business Cycle Variables** | | | | | | | | | | |
| Personal Income Growth (1-year lag) | -0.274 | ** | -0.270 | ** | -0.244 | ** | -0.324 | *** | -0.221 | * |
| | 0.109 | | 0.108 | | 0.113 | | 0.110 | | 0.114 | |
| Personal Income Growth ( 2-year lag) | -0.034 | | -0.033 | | -0.031 | | -0.072 | | -0.063 | |
| | 0.102 | | 0.102 | | 0.106 | | 0.105 | | 0.107 | |
| Personal Income Growth (Avg. 3-5 yr.) | 0.581 | *** | 0.579 | *** | 0.475 | *** | 0.578 | *** | 0.548 | *** |
| | 0.158 | | 0.1560 | | 0.162 | | 0.165 | | 0.162 | |
| Problem Bank % | 0.109 | *** | 0.108 | *** | 0.144 | *** | | | 0.110 | *** |
| | 0.028 | | 0.028 | | 0.029 | | | | 0.030 | |
| Failed Bank % | | | | | | | 0.058 | | | |
| | | | | | | | 0.053 | | | |
| Observations | 1307 | | 1307 | | 1307 | | 1307 | | 1349 | |
| R-Square | 0.463 | | 0.463 | | 0.417 | | 0.458 | | 0.420 | |
| Adjusted R-Square | 0.458 | | 0.458 | | 0.412 | | 0.453 | | 0.415 | |

Significance at the 10%, 5%, and 1% level is represented by *, **, *** respectively.

## Table 4

Regression Results for Loss Rate on Failed Bank Assets

| | 1<br>Coefficient<br>*Std. Error* | 2<br>Coefficient<br>*Std. Error* | 3<br>Coefficient<br>*Std. Error* | 4<br>Coefficient<br>*Std. Error* | 5<br>Coefficient<br>*Std. Error* |
|---|---|---|---|---|---|
| **Bank-Specific Variables** | | | | | |
| Intercept | 31.218 *** | 32.710 *** | 31.706 *** | 29.103 *** | 31.759 *** |
| | *3.492* | *3.498* | *3.508* | *3.762* | *3.486* |
| Log of Real Gross Assets | -2.378 *** | -2.049 *** | -2.369 *** | -2.396 *** | -2.413 *** |
| | *0.221* | *0.219* | *0.221* | *0.221* | *0.221* |
| Loans and Leases % of Assets | 0.108 *** | 0.125 *** | 0.106 *** | 0.104 *** | 0.104 *** |
| | *0.022* | *0.219* | *0.022* | *0.022* | *0.022* |
| Commercial and Industrial % of Loans | 0.072 *** | 0.069 *** | 0.072 *** | 0.072 *** | 0.074 *** |
| | *0.017* | *0.017* | *0.017* | *0.017* | *0.017* |
| Income Earned but Not Collected | 3.880 *** | 3.275 *** | 3.836 *** | 3.910 *** | 3.604 *** |
| | *0.348* | *0.343* | *0.350* | *0.349* | *0.360* |
| Other Real Estate Owned | 0.767 *** | 0.832 *** | 0.770 *** | 0.766 *** | 0.776 *** |
| | *0.060* | *0.060* | *0.060* | *0.060* | *0.060* |
| Core Deposits % of Liabilities | -0.122 *** | -0.149 *** | -0.121 *** | -0.117 *** | -0.117 *** |
| | *0.022* | *0.022* | *0.022* | *0.022* | *0.022* |
| Loan Loss Reserve Underfunding | -0.551 *** | -0.563 *** | -0.550 *** | -0.550 *** | -0.555 *** |
| | *0.039* | *0.039* | *0.039* | *0.039* | *0.039* |
| Avg. Asset Growth | 0.061 *** | 0.072 *** | 0.063 *** | 0.062 *** | 0.059 *** |
| | *0.017* | *0.017* | *0.017* | *0.017* | *0.017* |
| **Business Cycle Variables** | | | | | |
| Personal Income Growth (year of failure) | | | -0.172 | | |
| | | | *0.126* | | |
| Personal Income Growth (1-year lag) | -0.270 ** | | -0.218 * | -0.224 ** | -0.305 *** |
| | *0.108* | | *0.115* | *0.113* | *0.109* |
| Personal Income Growth ( 2-year lag) | -0.033 | | -0.069 | -0.037 | -0.154 |
| | *0.102* | | *0.105* | *0.102* | *0.110* |
| Personal Income Growth (Avg. 3-5 yr.) | 0.579 *** | | 0.578 *** | 0.603 *** | 0.474 *** |
| | *0.156* | | *0.156* | *0.157* | *0.160* |
| Unemployment (year of failure) | | | | 0.300 | |
| | | | | *0.199* | |
| Bankruptcy Growth (year of failure) | | | | | 0.063 *** |
| | | | | | *0.022* |
| Problem Bank % | 0.107 *** | | 0.100 *** | 0.101 *** | 0.098 *** |
| | *0.028* | | *0.029* | *0.029* | *0.028* |
| Observations | 1307 | 1307 | 1307 | 1307 | 1307 |
| R-Square | 0.463 | 0.442 | 0.464 | 0.464 | 0.467 |
| Adjusted R-Square | 0.458 | 0.439 | 0.459 | 0.459 | 0.461 |

Significance at the 10%, 5%, and 1% level is represented by *, **, *** respectively.

## Figure 1

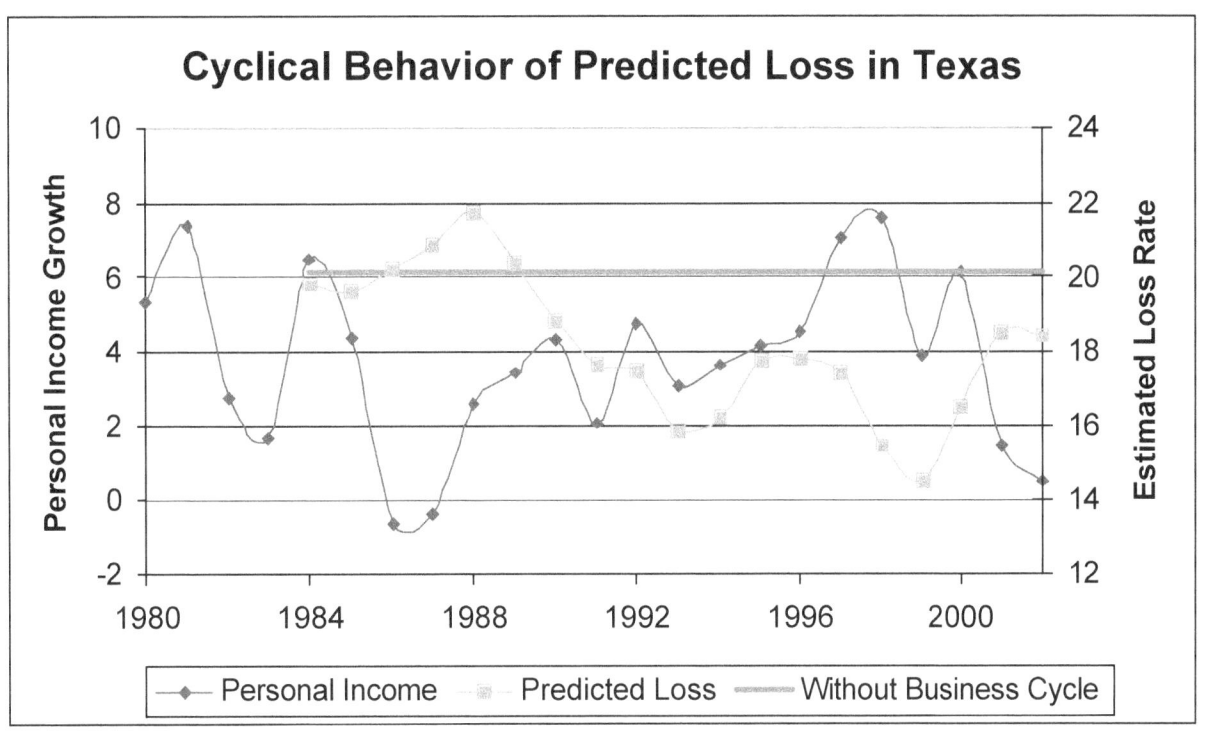

## Figure 2

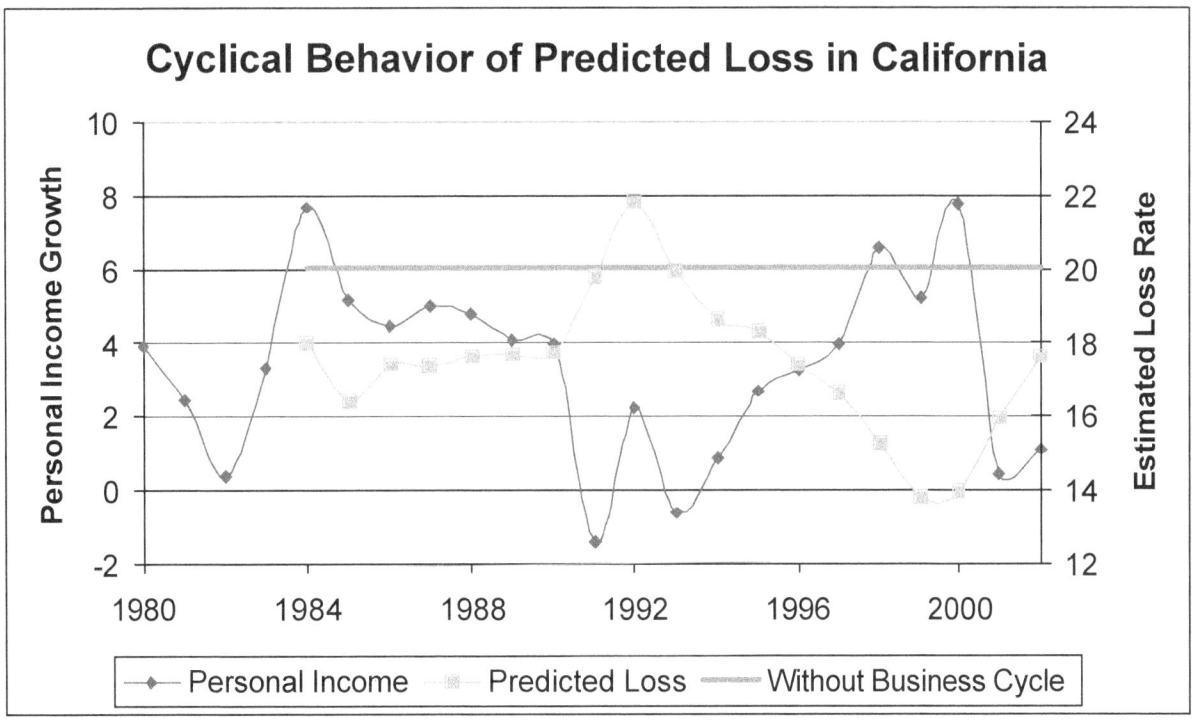

## References

Altman, Edward I., Brooks Brady, Andrea Resti and Andrea Sironi. 2002. The Link Between Default and Recovery Rates: Implications for Credit Risk Models and Procyclicality. Working Paper FIN-02-049, Department of Finance, NYU Stern School of Business.

Bernanke, Ben S. 1983. Nonmonetary Effects of the Financial Crisis in Propagation of the Great Depression. *American Economic Review* 73, no. 3: 257–76.

Bovenzi, John F., and Arthur J. Murton. 1988. Resolution Costs of Bank Failures. *FDIC Banking Review* 1, no.1: 1–13.

Brown, Richard A., and Seth Epstein. 1992. Resolution Costs of Bank Failures: An Update of the FDIC Historical Loss Model. *FDIC Banking Review* 5, no.1: 1–16.

Frye, Jon. 2000. Depressing Recoveries. *Risk Magazine*, November.

González-Hermosillo, Brenda. 1999. Determinates of Ex-Ante Banking System Distress: A Macro-Micro Empirical Exploration of Some Recent Episodes. Working Paper 99/33, International Monetary Fund.

Gup, Benton. 1995. *Targeting Fraud: Uncovering & Deterring Fraud in Financial Institutions.* McGraw-Hill.

James, Christopher. 1992. The Losses Realized in Bank Failures. *The Journal of Finance* 46, no. 4: 1223–1242.

Jordan, John S., and Eric S. Rosengren. 2002. Economic Cycles and Bank Health. In *Conference Proceedings: The Impact of Economic Slowdowns on Financial Institutions and Their Regulators*. Federal Reserve Bank of Boston.

Kaminsky, Graciela L., and Carmen M. Reinhart. 1999. The Twin Crises: The Causes of Banking and Balance-of-Payments Problems. *American Economic Review* 89, no.3: 473–500.

Kaufman, George G. 2001. Macro-Economic Stability and Bank Soundness. Working Paper, 04/01/2001. Loyola University.

Nuxoll, Daniel A., John O'Keefe, and Katherine Samolyk. 2003. Do Local Economic Data Improve Off-Site Bank-Monitoring Models? *FDIC Banking Review* 15, no. 2: 39–53.

Osterberg, William P., and James B. Thomson. 1995. Underlying Determinants of Closed-Bank Resolution Costs. In *The Causes and Costs of Depository Institution Failures*, ed. Allin F. Cottrell, Michael S. Lawlor, and John H. Wood, 75–92. Kluwer Academic Publishers.

Salmon, Richard, Lisa Allston, Jeanne McBride, Dennis Trimper, Elvis Nelson, Debbie Barr, Beth Almond, Gwen Hudson, Donna Kinser, and Vicki Robinson. 2003. Costs Associated with Bank Failures. Unpublished paper, presented at the FDIC and Southern Methodist University Symposium: Lessons Learned from Bank Failures, Dallas.